D0742755

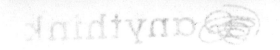

# ECO-DISASTERS

# POISONED AIR

## BHOPAL, INDIA

## by Meish Goldish

Consultant: International Campaign for Justice in Bhopal (ICJB)

### BEARPORT
#### PUBLISHING

New York, New York

## Credits

Cover and Title Page, © Nathan King/Alamy Stock Photo; 5T, © Prakash Hatvalne/Polaris/Newscom; 5B, © REUTERS/Alamy Stock Photo; 6, © dbimages/Alamy Stock Photo; 7, © Prakash Hatvalne/Polaris/Newscom; 8, © CRS PHOTO/Shutterstock; 9, © REUTERS/Alamy Stock Photo; 10, © Doreen Fiedler/dpa/picture-alliance/Newscom; 11T, © gvictoria/iStock; 11B, © molekuul_be/Shutterstock; 12, © Julian Nitzsche/tinyurl.com/lpxp6ld/CC BY-SA 3.0; 13, © Spencer Wynn; 14, © Nathan King/Alamy Stock Photo; 15T, © David Lichtneker/Alamy Stock Photo; 15B, © Automobus/Shutterstock; 16, © Hindustan Times/Newscom; 17, © BEDI/AFP/Getty Images; 18, © AP Photo/Sondeep Shankar, File; 19T, © SANJEEV GUPTA/EPA/Newscom; 19B, © AFP/Getty Images; 20, © Prakash Hatvalne/Polaris/Newscom; 21, © BEDI/AFP/Getty Images; 22, © Bhopal Medical Appeal/tinyurl.com/lsnzgar/CC BY-SA 2.0; 23, © Jack Laurenson/Bhopal Medical Appeal; 24, © Jack Laurenson/Bhopal Medical Appeal; 25T, © Jack Laurenson/Bhopal Medical Appeal; 25B, © SANJEEV GUPTA/EPA/Newscom; 26, © arindambanerjee/Shutterstock; 27T, © arindambanerjee/Shutterstock; 27B, © arindambanerjee/Shutterstock; 28, © arindambanerjee/Shutterstock; 29T, © AP Photo/Paul Sakuma; 29B, © Prakash Hatvalne/Polaris/Newscom; 31, © dbimages/Alamy Stock Photo.

Publisher: Kenn Goin
Editor: Jessica Rudolph
Creative Director: Spencer Brinker
Photo Researcher: Editorial Directions, Inc.

*Library of Congress Cataloging-in-Publication Data*

Names: Goldish, Meish, author.
Title: Poisoned air : Bhopal, India / by Meish Goldish.
Description: New York, New York : Bearport Publishing, 2018. | Series:
   Eco-disasters | Includes bibliographical references and index. | Audience:
   Age 5 to 8.
Identifiers: LCCN 2017005093 (print) | LCCN 2017012077 (ebook) | ISBN
   9781684022755 (ebook) | ISBN 9781684022212 (library)
Subjects: LCSH: Bhopal Union Carbide Plant Disaster, Bhopal, India,
   1984—Juvenile literature. | Chemical
   plants—Accidents—India—Bhopal—Juvenile literature. | Chemical
   plants—Accidents—Environmental aspects—Juvenile literature. | Methyl
   isocyanate—Toxicology—India—Bhopal—Juvenile literature.
Classification: LCC HD7269.C452 (ebook) | LCC HD7269.C452 I52427 2018 (print)
   | DDC 363.17/9109543—dc23
LC record available at https://lccn.loc.gov/2017005093

For more information, write to Bearport Publishing Company, Inc., 45 West 21st Street, Suite 3B, New York, New York 10010. Printed in the United States of America.

10 9 8 7 6 5 4 3 2 1

# Contents

# Night of Horror

December 2, 1984, was a chilly night in Bhopal, India. Most of the city's **residents** were asleep when, suddenly, they awoke gasping for breath. Aziza Sultan remembers: "About 12:30 a.m, I woke to the sound of my baby coughing badly. The room was filled with a white cloud. I heard people shouting, 'Run! Run!' Then I started coughing. It seemed as if I was breathing in fire. My eyes were burning."

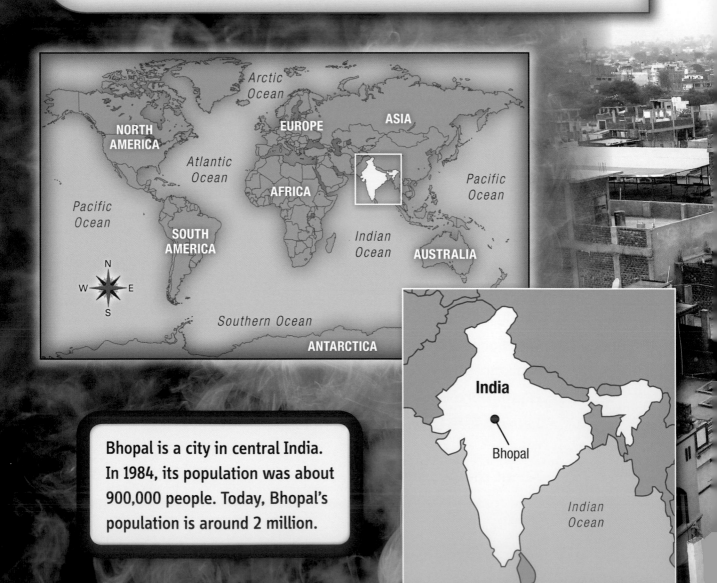

Bhopal is a city in central India. In 1984, its population was about 900,000 people. Today, Bhopal's population is around 2 million.

Across the city, hundreds of thousands of people were experiencing the same terror. In a **panic**, parents grabbed their children and rushed into the streets. They ran, not knowing what was happening. All around them, people and animals were collapsing and dying. What was causing this unbelievable horror?

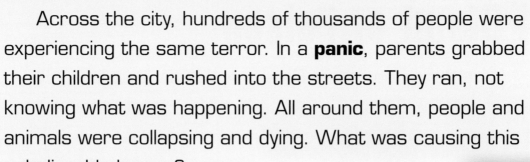

A woman with her dead cattle

A neighborhood in Bhopal

# A Cloud of Poison

Aziza Sultan and other Bhopal residents later learned that the white cloud they had seen in their homes and in the streets was a deadly gas called methyl isocyanate, or MIC. It came from a nearby **chemical** factory run by an American company called the Union Carbide Corporation (UCC).

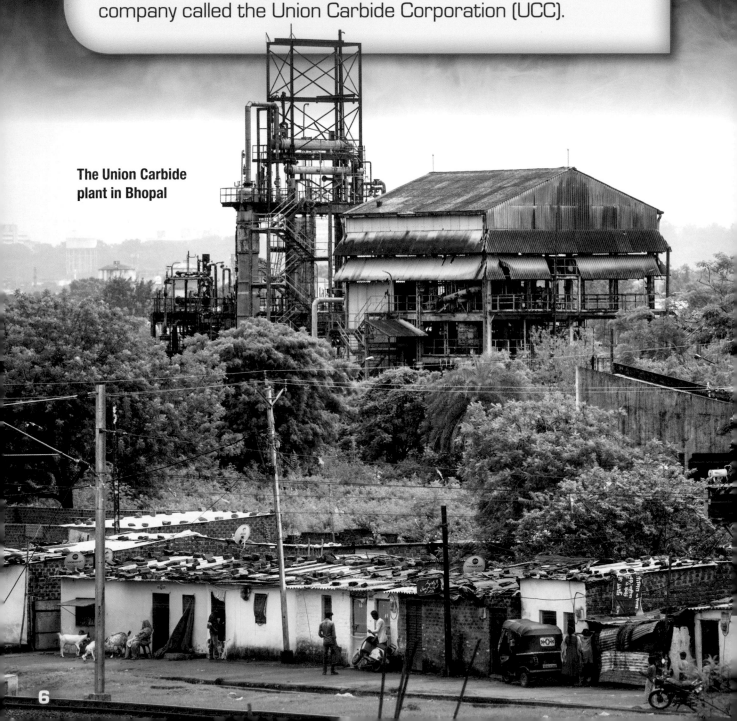

**The Union Carbide plant in Bhopal**

That December night, a terrible disaster occurred at the factory. Plumes of poisonous MIC gas leaked into the air. About 600,000 residents of Bhopal breathed in the poison. Within three days of the disaster, 8,000 to 10,000 **victims** died. Their bodies littered the streets. Hundreds of thousands more became seriously ill.

MIC is heavier than air, so when the gas floats freely, it stays close to the ground.

Thousands of victims who breathed the poisonous gas died in the streets.

# Business Gone Bad

The tragedy in Bhopal first began in 1969, when UCC built a chemical plant in the city. The plant made **pesticides** to sell to farmers throughout India. The chemicals helped increase **crop** production by killing insects that harmed plants.

Indian farmers grow crops such as corn, wheat, soybeans, and rice. Here, a farmer sprays pesticides on soybeans.

UCC built the chemical factory in Bhopal because the city is in the center of India. The location made it easier for the company to ship its products all over the country.

At first, the pesticides sold well. However, in the early 1980s, **droughts** destroyed much of the farmland in India. As a result, crops grew poorly, and Indian farmers made very little money. They could no longer afford to buy the pesticides. With slow sales, the UCC factory was soon losing money.

An Indian farmer and his water buffalo in a drought-stricken field

# Cutting Back on Safety

During the droughts, UCC looked for ways to save money at its factory in Bhopal. The company cut back sharply on the number of its employees. For example, the **maintenance** crew went from six workers to just two. UCC also reduced the amount of safety training each worker received from six months to just 15 days. In addition, when safety equipment at the plant broke, it was not repaired.

T.R. Chouhan, a former UCC employee, stands in front of equipment from the old factory building.

UCC saved money in another way, too. One of the main ingredients the company used to make pesticides was MIC. Other pesticide companies had stopped using MIC because it was dangerous to work with. However, UCC kept using the ingredient because it cost less than other chemicals.

Many pesticides contain dangerous chemicals and must be handled properly.

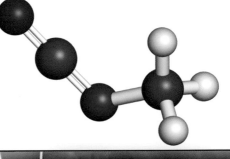

This is an illustration of an MIC molecule. It's made up of one oxygen (red), two carbon (black), one nitrogen (blue), and three hydrogen (white) atoms.

UCC workers complained about the dangerous conditions and warned of a possible disaster. However, **managers** ignored their concerns.

# Gas Leak!

The factory workers' fears of a disaster came true on the night of December 2, 1984. At the plant, there was 60 tons (54 metric tons) of liquid MIC stored in a large tank. A worker was told to use water to clean the buildup of solid MIC in the pipes connected to the tank.

This old storage tank was once used to hold MIC at the Union Carbide Corporation plant.

However, the **valves** in the pipes were **defective** and leaking, so the water used for washing started to flow into the MIC tank. When the MIC and water mixed, a chemical reaction occurred. The temperature inside the tank rose, and the liquid MIC turned into gas. The pressure increased, and safety equipment designed to keep the gas inside the tank broke. Suddenly, the gas burst out and tons of poisonous MIC escaped into the air!

A pipe connected to a tank at the former UCC plant

MIC is poisonous in all states—solid, liquid, and gas.

# Panic at the Plant

When the MIC gas drifted into the air, some workers at the plant panicked and ran for their lives. Others stayed behind and tried to turn on safety equipment that was meant to control a gas leak. None of the equipment worked because it had been broken for months.

Some workers abandoned the control room and other parts of the factory when the leak occurred.

A loud warning siren soon went off at the factory, but plant managers quickly shut it down to prevent the people of Bhopal from panicking. Even if the siren had kept wailing, residents would not have had an escape plan. UCC officials never taught them what to do if poisonous gas escaped into the city.

Residents of Bhopal

Warning sirens at the plant had gone off many times in the past because of less serious gas leaks. Yet most residents of Bhopal didn't know what the sirens were meant to warn them about.

# Hospital Havoc

The cloud of poison, blown by the wind, spread across an area of about 15 square miles (39 sq km) and soon reached Bhopal's residents. As they breathed in the gas, it burned their lungs and stung their eyes. Thousands of victims, barely able to see, ran to the nearest hospitals. Some stumbled and fell along the way. Many died when the MIC caused their lungs to fill with fluid.

Rows of people who died from breathing the poisonous gas

At the hospitals, doctors and nurses saw patients with swollen eyes. Many were coughing and foaming at the mouth. One doctor, D.K. Satpathy, saw a man struggling to breathe. "After a while, that person died and I couldn't understand what happened to him, because I did not know which gas had leaked." Even when doctors later learned that the people had been poisoned by MIC, they were unsure how to treat the problem. UCC had not given the doctors proper instructions on how to treat MIC **exposure**.

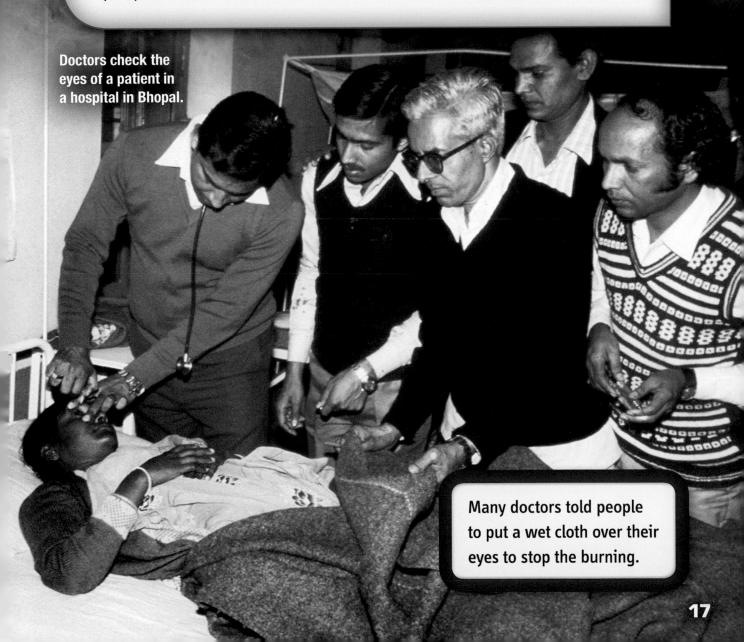

Doctors check the eyes of a patient in a hospital in Bhopal.

Many doctors told people to put a wet cloth over their eyes to stop the burning.

# From Bad to Worse

In the days after the leak, the situation in Bhopal grew worse. Thousands more people died from the aftereffects of breathing in the poison. Some died when the poison damaged their **vital organs**, including their lungs, kidneys, and livers. Others who had fallen on their way to the hospital died from their injuries days later.

Many family members got separated during the **chaos** of the gas leak and searched for one another.

About 600,000 people who had survived suffered from various injuries and illnesses. Many had damaged eyes or were unable to walk. Others grew **depressed** over losing family members. One survivor, Rashida Bi, lost five relatives. "Those who escaped with their lives are the unlucky ones," she said. "The lucky ones are those who died on that night."

These victims suffered damage to their eyes from the gas leak.

This man's relative died during the disaster.

# Dealing with the Dead

On top of everything, the thousands of **corpses** in Bhopal created a health **hazard** for the city. Bodies of people and animals had to be **disposed** of quickly to prevent the spread of disease. Survivors took care of the bodies of family members in different ways. Hindus burned their dead, according to the rules of their religion. Muslims dug deep graves that held several bodies, one on top of the other.

Machines had to be used to remove and bury the heaviest animals, such as these water buffalo.

Because of the need to act quickly, funerals for one victim at a time were not possible. Instead, there were mass funerals and **cremations**. A photographer named Raghu Rai arrived in Bhopal the day after the disaster and began taking pictures of the tragedy. He said, "It was like . . . an earthquake had just finished and people were trying to recover their dead . . . There were so many dead bodies coming, and there were so few people who were handling it."

A family prepares a dead relative for cremation.

On orders from government officials, many bodies lying in the streets were taken by city truck drivers and dumped into a nearby river.

# Who's to Blame?

After the disaster, people in India were outraged—and they wanted answers. Government officials blamed UCC for not running its plant safely. They said the MIC should have been stored at a cooler temperature. Because it was stored improperly, the chemical reaction of the water and the MIC was very fast. This led to the temperature and pressure of the MIC in the tank rising quickly, creating conditions for a deadly gas leak.

MIC must be kept at a temperature of 41°F (5°C) or lower to remain safe.

However, UCC officials argued that their plant was safe. They claimed that an unhappy worker at the factory had forced water into the MIC tank to purposely cause a gas leak in order to harm the company. However, UCC never provided **evidence** for this claim, and it's believed to be untrue.

In a **settlement** with the Indian government in 1989, UCC paid the disaster victims $470 million. That came to the very small sum of about $2,200 for the family of each dead victim and only about $500 for each injured victim.

It was discovered that UCC had shut off cooling equipment for the MIC months before the gas leak to save money on electricity.

# Ignoring the Problem

After the gas leak, UCC's pesticide plant in Bhopal was shut down. However, the damage caused by the plant went far beyond the terrible leak and its immediate aftermath. **Investigators** found that during the 15 years before the disaster, deadly chemicals from the plant had **seeped** into the ground and into the city's water system.

The chemical plant in Bhopal still stands today, rotting away more than 30 years after it closed.

Today, the chemicals are still in the ground, and the water continues to poison Bhopal's residents. In recent years, poisonous chemicals have also been found in the milk of mothers **nursing** their babies. Even with this new knowledge, no cleanup of Bhopal's water or land has ever taken place.

Today, many residents of Bhopal still drink the poisoned water because they don't have access to clean water.

In 2001, an American company called Dow Chemical bought UCC. Dow officials claim that since they never operated the pesticide plant in Bhopal, they aren't responsible for cleaning up the land or water there.

Many people in Bhopal demand that Dow help remove the hazardous chemicals in the land and water.

# The Nightmare Continues

The disaster still haunts the city of Bhopal to this day. Victims continue to die or suffer from illnesses related to the gas leak. Even people born after 1984 have been affected. Many girls who survived the poisonous gas grew up to give birth to children with brain damage or physical **deformities**. Other children have developed cancer. These problems are linked to the gas and to the poisoned water.

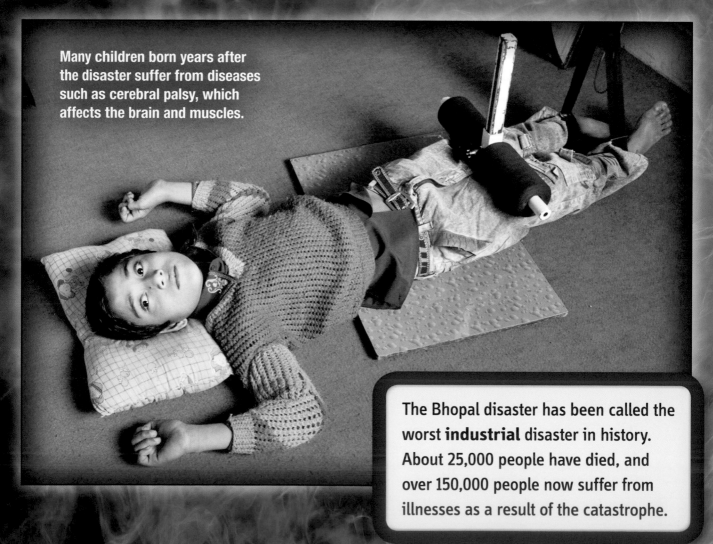

Many children born years after the disaster suffer from diseases such as cerebral palsy, which affects the brain and muscles.

The Bhopal disaster has been called the worst **industrial** disaster in history. About 25,000 people have died, and over 150,000 people now suffer from illnesses as a result of the catastrophe.

Today, many survivors feel helpless. Shaqur Ali can't work because of serious breathing problems. He spends the little money he has on medicine. "I am alive, but I am like a dead person," he said. "I often think my life is useless." Facing similar hardships, other struggling victims in Bhopal hope for a brighter future for themselves, their families, and their city.

The people of Bhopal hold protests in the hopes that their situation will improve.

This statue, which shows a mother and child, honors the victims of the Bhopal gas disaster.

# Fixing the Future

Since the Bhopal disaster of 1984, efforts have been made to help the many victims who still suffer. Here are some examples.

Patients waiting at Sambhavna Trust

## Medical Care

Many organizations were started to help survivors affected by the tragedy. The Sambhavna Trust runs a health clinic that provides free medical treatment for MIC survivors and for residents who have been exposed to the chemically poisoned water. The Chingari Trust gives free medical care to children in Bhopal who were born with brain damage and physical deformities.

## Looking for Justice

Bhopal survivors have gone to court to demand punishment for former UCC executives. Their claim is that the inaction and **negligence** of these officials led to violations in safety standards at the Bhopal plant, which caused the gas leak disaster. Survivors hope that bringing the officials to justice will prevent similar disasters from occurring in the future.

**Rashida Bi and Champa Devi Shukla**

## Activists

There are many activists in India who work for the rights of the survivors. Rashida Bi and Champa Devi Shukla organize rallies that call attention to the victims. They try to get the Indian government to clean up the city's unhealthy water supply and to demand money from Dow Chemical for the gas victims.

## Around the World

Thousands of people take part in protest marches in countries around the world. These actions call attention to the Bhopal disaster survivors and their need for more money, since many of the victims are no longer able to work.

# Glossary

**chaos** (KAY-ahs) total confusion

**chemical** (KEM-uh-kuhl) a man-made substance that can sometimes be harmful to living things

**corpses** (KORPS-iz) dead bodies

**cremations** (kree-MAY-shuhnz) the burning of dead bodies to ashes

**crop** (KROP) a plant that is grown in large quantities on a farm, usually for food

**defective** (dih-FEK-tiv) having a fault or weakness

**deformities** (dih-FORM-uh-teez) conditions in which a body is twisted, bent, or disfigured

**depressed** (dih-PREST) very sad

**disposed** (diss-POHZD) gotten rid of

**droughts** (DROUTS) long periods of time with little or no rain

**evidence** (EV-uh-duhnss) information and facts that help give proof of something

**exposure** (eks-POH-shur) the state of being in contact with something dangerous

**hazard** (HAZ-urd) something that may be very dangerous

**industrial** (in-DUHSS-tree-uhl) having to do with factories or businesses

**investigators** (in-VESS-tuh-gay-turz) people who conduct a thorough study of something, such as a crime

**maintenance** (MAYN-tuh-nuhnss) the upkeep of property or equipment

**managers** (MAN-uh-jurz) people who oversee groups of employees in a business

**negligence** (NEG-luh-jenss) a failure to provide proper care, which may lead to the injury or death of people who lack protection

**nursing** (NURS-ing) feeding a baby with a mother's milk

**panic** (PAN-ik) a sudden feeling of fright or terror

**pesticides** (PESS-tuh-sidez) chemicals used to kill insects and other pests that damage crops

**residents** (REZ-uh-duhnss) people who live in a particular place

**seeped** (SEEPT) flowed or trickled slowly

**settlement** (SET-uhl-muhnt) a legal agreement

**valves** (VALVZ) movable parts that control the flow of a liquid or gas through pipes or other passageways

**victims** (VIK-tuhmz) people or animals who are hurt or killed in an accident or disaster

**vital organs** (VYE-tuhl ORE-guhnz) parts of the body, such as the brain, lungs, and liver, that are needed to keep a person alive

# Bibliography

**D'Silva, Themistocles.** *The Black Box of Bhopal: A Closer Look at the World's Deadliest Industrial Disaster.* Victoria, BC, Canada: Trafford (2006).

**Lapierre, Dominique, and Javier Moro.** *Five Past Midnight in Bhopal.* New York: Warner Books (2002).

**Mukherjee, Suroopa.** *Surviving Bhopal: Dancing Bodies, Written Texts, and Oral Testimonials of Women in the Wake of an Industrial Disaster.* New York: Palgrave Macmillan (2010).

**Pietersen, Chris.** *The Two Largest Industrial Disasters in History with Hazardous Material.* New Delhi, India: KW Publishers (2014).

# Read More

**Bryan, Nichol.** *Bhopal: Chemical Plant Accident (Environmental Disasters).* Milwaukee, WI: World Almanac Library (2004).

**Riddle, John.** *Bhopal (Great Disasters: Reforms and Ramifications).* Philadelphia: Chelsea House (2002).

# Learn More Online

To learn more about the Bhopal gas leak disaster, visit
**www.bearportpublishing.com/EcoDisasters**

# Index

# About the Author

Meish Goldish has written more than 300 books for children. His book *City Firefighters* won a Teachers' Choice Award in 2015. He lives in Brooklyn, New York.